Think & Grow Wealthy
The Hidden Psychology to Prosperity & Abundance

By

Robert Heng

DEDICATION

I dedicate *Think & Growth Wealthy* to the pride and joy of my life, my two beautiful daughters, Brittany and Gabriella, and to my beautiful wife, Jodie, all of whom mean the world to me. It was through them that I drew the strength to finish this work so that I might be able to try to help others find their true meaning of wealth, prosperity, abundance, and fulfillment in their lives as they all helped me find it in mine.

When I started on this journey to write this book, I had no idea at the time that I would encounter the challenges I did and that these challenges would dramatically alter my life, plans, and dreams from what I had intended.

In the end, it was my family support and the strong desire to produce something of tangible value for others that kept me pressing forward. It was also a reminder that you must live each and every day as if it were your last because someday you will be right!

I want to also thank Dr. Matthew James with the Empowerment Partnership (http://www.nlp.com), whose teachings broadened my passion and enlightenment in the field of neuro-linguistic-programming (NLP). NLP is truly an amazing and empowering field of study, building a greater understanding of one's self to become a better communicator with yourself and others. The study and practice of NLP, as well as Dr. James' lessons, provided me with the strength and understanding that how you decide to live your life always remains a personal choice.

There is no better, more rewarding feeling than coming to understand yourself in a deeper, more vibrant way so that you can help others discover their true, though many times hidden, potential.

I hope that by the time you have read this book, you, too, will have discovered a hidden passion, first for yourself and then for others.

My true desire and prayers are that you learn to live your life for all it's worth and find the strength and wisdom to work because you want to, not because you have to. Enjoy your life, and help those around you celebrate with you.

Practice random acts of kindness, and never lose sight of the gift of giving, whether it's of your money, time, or service. Be grateful for what you have, and always live in the moment because you never know what tomorrow will bring.

You can make a difference in the world, but it must start with you and your world. Strive to understand, accept, and practice how you can transform your life to Think & Grow Wealthy.

INTRODUCTION

You want "wealth"; maybe you already consider yourself "wealthy," but something just isn't right in your life. It's more than just money; in fact, it's never been just about money. You're looking all around for the help you so desperately believe you need. You've looked everywhere except the obvious place—you haven't learned to look to yourself.

In today's world, balancing your work life with your personal life is harder than ever. We end up working so hard to get ahead that we forget or miss the critically important events in our lives that really mean more than money.

In this book, I am going to show you why you tend to miss those important events and why it matters to you from a true wealth perspective. By learning and practicing the lessons learned in this book, you will become the master of your behavior instead of a slave to it. You will learn the secrets behind the *Hidden Psychology* to becoming *Wealthy* and achieving prosperity and abundance.

This book is for those who want more in life than just a number representing a net worth or funds on deposit at a bank. It's for people who suffer from procrastination and commitment to themselves and to the ones that mean the most in their lives.

As someone who has dedicated my life to the service of others in one form or another, I take you by the hand and share with you the passion of self-discovery and how it is so vitally important to your success in creating, finding, building, and enjoying wealth and prosperity.

This book helps you find your solution—one that is tailored to you and only you because it is derived from your true values.

I promise that if you follow and practice the lessons and teachings of this book, you will find new meaning for the word "wealth." It will be a meaning that brings you prosperity, abundance, and fulfillment in a way you never dreamed possible.

Don't be the person who misses out, especially if you have loved ones that depend on your commitment to your and their overall wellbeing and happiness. Time is a wasting resource, and in the field of financial services, it is the one valuable asset that can never be replaced.

Be the person who others say about, "I don't know how they do it." Be the kind of person who takes positive action and does so immediately.

The personal productivity teachings and lessons you're about to read have been proven to create positive, long-lasting, life-changing results. All you have to do to stay in control of your passage to true ecological wealth is to keep reading.

Take control of your life right now, make it productive, and enjoy the new life you're creating. You won't believe the change within yourself, in your feelings, in your outlook, and in your fulfillment.

PREFACE

This book is not a heavy lift, and I kept it short in an effort to encourage not only its initial reading but also its re-reading in order to fully understand the concepts that are introduced.

It is designed to get you to **THINK** in order to learn more about yourself so that you can fully and completely sustain forward motion on your passage to **prosperity** and **abundance**.

On June 12, 2005, Steve Jobs delivered a Commencement address at Stanford University. At the time, Steve knew he was dying, and his message was one that resounds throughout this book.

We all know that Steve had a lot of money, but it's not until you read and understand his message that you come to appreciate the level of true wealth and prosperity he had achieved. It's never the amount the money but rather it's always about your life and how you decide to live it. On that June day in 2005, Steve Jobs delivered the following message:

Steve started his address with an unsourced quote*: "If you live each day as if it was your last, someday you'll most certainly be right. It made an impression on me, and since then, for the past 33 years, I have looked in the mirror every morning and asked myself: 'If today were the last day of my life, would I want to do what I am about to do today?' And whenever the answer has been 'No' for too many* *days in a row, I know I need to change something.*

Remembering that I'll be dead soon is the most important tool I've ever encountered to help me make the big choices in life. Because almost everything—all external expectations, all pride, all fear of embarrassment or failure—these things just fall away in the face of death, leaving only what is truly important. Remembering that you are going to die is the best way I know to avoid the trap of thinking you have something to lose. You are already naked. There is no reason not to follow your heart.

About a year ago I was diagnosed with cancer. I had a scan at 7:30 in the morning, and it clearly showed a tumor on my pancreas. I didn't even know what a pancreas was. The doctors told me this was almost certainly a type of cancer that is incurable and that I should expect to live no longer than three to six months. My doctor advised me to go home and get my affairs in order, which is doctor's code for prepare to die. It means to try to tell your kids everything you thought you'd have the next 10 years to tell them in just a few months. It means to make sure everything is buttoned up so that it will be as easy as possible for your family. It means to say your goodbyes.

I lived with that diagnosis all day. Later that evening I had a biopsy, where they stuck an endoscope down my throat, through my stomach and into my intestines, put a needle into my pancreas and got a few cells from the tumor. I was sedated, but my wife, who was there, told me that when they viewed the cells under a microscope the doctors started crying because it turned out to be a very rare form of pancreatic cancer that is curable with surgery. I had the surgery and I'm fine now.

This was the closest I've been to facing death, and I hope it's the closest I get for a few more decades. Having lived through it, I can now say this to you with a bit more certainty than when death was a useful but purely intellectual concept:

No one wants to die. Even people who want to go to heaven don't want to die to get there. And yet death is the destination we all share. No one has ever escaped it. And that is as it should be, because Death is very likely the single best invention of Life. It is Life's change agent. It clears out the old to make way for the new. Right now the new is you, but someday not too long from now, you will gradually become the old and be cleared away. Sorry to be so dramatic, but it is quite true.

Your time is limited, so don't waste it living someone else's life. Don't be trapped by dogma—which is living with the results of other people's thinking. Don't let the noise of others' opinions drown out your own inner voice. And most important, have the courage to follow your heart and intuition. They somehow already know what you truly want to become. Everything else is secondary."

Everything we construct, produce, or create affects our lives and the lives of those around us. Before we're able to construct, produce, or create, we must first **think**, so it's our thoughts that hold the key to our disappointment and sadness as well as our success and happiness.

Most don't realize that it's your subconscious mind that controls your conscious thoughts and that it's responsible for about 90% of your daily behavior and actions. Learning how and why you think the way you do is critical to your ultimate success in life and in wealth.

Learning how you can become a better thinker and communicator with yourself and others will empower you to find, create, retain, and enjoy a life of wealth, prosperity, abundance, and fulfillment.

Our biggest challenges in life boils down to our relationships, our health, and our finances. There must be harmony between all three in order to produce abundance and fulfillment.

I wrote this book for you because it became a logical extension for my passion to help and serve others where and how I can.

My first true passion in life was sports and baseball in particular. Although I always thought that someday I might make it to the professional ranks, injuries and a lack of exceptional talent forced me to accept my true limitations and change paths.

I decided to follow my fascination of science and study oceanography with hopes of someday discovering the key to unlocking the secrets of using salt water to germinate crops in order to feed a starving planet.

It was a noble goal, but like my dreams of playing baseball, it, too, was short-lived. The reason I let myself down in this endeavor was the unfortunate timing of a time-intensive botany lab in the springtime. While I loved the ocean, so did my classmates, and the beaches, bikinis, and good times took their toll.

In search of a new passion, I soon discovered the field of public service through law enforcement. Well, actually, law enforcement found me (that's another story altogether).

The experience intrigued me, and I immediately knew what I wanted to do with my life.. Fast forward about thirty years into that career when I began to plan and envision what I might like to do next. I knew whatever it was, it had to involve some level of service to others in order to provide a sense of security and attainment to not only myself but to others as well.

So while still serving in my law enforcement capacity, I decided to study and enter the field of the financial services industry, where I trained and practiced from 1996 to the present. While still working full time in law enforcement, I helped friends and colleagues construct and manage their investments.

I wanted to help them enrich their fortunes any way I could while honing my abilities to effectively manage personal financial assets for when I retired from my full-time law enforcement profession.

I continue to provide contract consulting services to the law enforcement community on complex financial crimes using interviewing techniques and building rapport. I also continue my work as a registered investment advisor representative, managing personal portfolios and continuing to help others work toward and attain their dreams of financial freedom.

It was while working with those in the public service sector that I discovered many work just because they have to, not necessarily because they want to.

Far too often the services of professional money management were out of their reach as retirement savings fell well short of the minimums required by many in the financial services industry.

As a result, many were left to fend for themselves and fell prey to monthly investment publications touting the "best" stock or mutual fund to own long term only to be replaced by the next best "stock or mutual fund" the following month.

These civil servants found themselves not only priced out of the services of financial professionals, but they were enticed to chase past performance in hopes of leveraging their existing savings— believing net worth defined true wealth.

I enjoyed tremendous success while working in the law enforcement field, and it wasn't until I discovered the field of neuro-linguistic-programing (NLP) that I realized why and how I had achieved that level of success in dealing with others, including many who were in deep stress and conflicted in their lives—on both sides of the law. I had an undiscovered subconscious ability to establish rapport and help many of them find hope and direction, which was astonishingly rewarding.

It was only through my discovery and later studies of NLP that I discovered the true secrets of what allowed me to be successful, although at the time, I had no idea why or how I was achieving the results that I and others were witnessing.

I knew I had to take all of my life's experience and training to find a way to give back and help as many people as I could, so I created a platform through which I could help others in discovering more about themselves so they could build choices to create a greater sense of wealth and prosperity.

To me, the field of NLP involves the art of communication and becoming a better communicator with myself and others. It involves understanding that my ability to communicate intentions is dependent on understanding my own internal map of my world and that unless I can recognize and associate to others, I have to rely on their actions as feedback that my intentions were adequately expressed. Once we are congruent with each other's responses, we have achieved rapport, and true communication can advance.

When I decided to pursue an education and career in the financial services industry, I did so because of a desire to help others build and find financial stability, abundance, and success. True wealth was never an intention because I had yet to discover within myself what wealthy truly meant.

My principal audience was the law enforcement community because that's who I knew, and I knew how dedicated they were to helping others solve life's vital challenges. Their passions to service often meant neglecting their own financial security and wellbeing.

It was my way of trying to educate them and help them and their families enjoy some level of financial fulfillment at the end of a stressful and often dangerous career.

I continue on this journey in life, still on the path of trying to help others, armed with the knowledge and understanding of how and why we do the things we do and, more importantly, don't do.

I'm able to continue in my service to others by helping others to find the wealth they seek and to do it through helping them identify their true values. In this way, they can achieve greater flexibility, choices, empowerment, and fulfillment, creating an ecological wealth involving prosperity and abundance.

Accept that there are no meaningful shortcuts, and commit to your learning.

You must also be willing to open your mind and be receptive to changing the way you *think* so that you can discover certain mindsets and beliefs that actually limit your behavior and ability to take action in order to achieve your goals and desired outcomes.

If you keep an open mind and truly make an effort to understand and practice the concepts being presented, you will find that you always have the resources available to make the changes and develop the results that you sought all along.

You just weren't consciously aware that your subconscious held the secrets and just needed your permission to guide your conscious mind to achieve your goals and dreams.

Promise me you will begin this journey and passage with a desire to learn more about yourself and those you care most deeply for. It will keep you motivated, and you will learn more about yourself than you ever realized possible.

As we make our way through this journey together, **you will discover more about yourself**. The more you learn, the more you'll realize you don't know.

Hopefully you will become a little confused, because your confusion means you're learning and associating that new knowledge to preexisting or preconceived notions, which creates and drives your internal conflict—thus confusion.

That education will drive you forward and inspire you to identify and define your true goals and objectives so that when you identify them, you can fully attain them.

You will enjoy a greater sense of true fulfillment because you will have harmonized your goals and intentions with your true values.

While I will venture into areas of traditional "investing" and personal finance, this book is not meant or designed to provide any significant measure of advice on how someone should construct or manage their investment portfolios or what you should specifically invest in to increase or achieve any level of financial diversification or "success."

"Success" is such a subjective descriptor and means something entirely different to each individual. Without knowing about your specific financial goals, risk tolerances, or time horizon, recommending specific asset allocations, investment vehicles, or asset classes would be inappropriate and irresponsible.

It is, however, designed to assist you in becoming a better communicator with yourself and others so that you will develop the knowledge, skills, and ability to create a greater level of personal empowerment.

You will find that you are able to use that empowerment to make better, more informed decisions about your personal finances— **giving you the opportunity to find your path to true values**.

This will lead to greater wealth and prosperity because it will allow you to see and remove obstacles or **limiting beliefs** that have resulted in **limiting decisions** that have greatly impacted your financial success and ecological wealth.

Far too many people let their limited understanding of money drive and enslave them. It's critically important that you break those chains and become the **master of money and true wealth and to not let money or your drive for financial freedom master you**.

You do this yourself by becoming more resourceful and having a more meaningful life through gaining greater flexibility and achieving prosperity, abundance, and a true, meaningful fulfillment of life. These are powerful and empowering concepts to master.

Does that sound like something that might be of value to you in your life?

Good, then keep reading to learn the keys to unlocking the mysteries of personal empowerment along your amazing journey to wealth, fulfillment, prosperity, and abundance. Once you reach your well-defined goals and objectives of true ecological wealth, you will find yourself at a place where you work because you want to and not because you have to. That's empowerment!

I start by sharing with you the process and belief that certain assumptions are presupposed to be true. You don't need to believe these presuppositions in order to test their usefulness. You just need to act as if they were true in order to notice the amazing empowerment and results you will achieve.

Remember, **don't prejudge them**; let them sink in, question them in your mind, and let them have meaning for you for they hold the keys to your journey to true wealth, prosperity, fulfillment, and abundance.

As we get ready to jump off on this wonderful journey together, take a moment to reflect on the words of William Ward: **"Before you speak, listen. Before you write, think. Before you spend, earn. Before you invest, investigate. Before you criticize, wait. Before you pray, forgive. Before you quit, try. Before you retire, save. Before you die, give."**

Now let's begin this magical journey and passage as you discover your true meaning of wealth, prosperity, and abundance. **It's time to Think & Grow Wealthy!**

TABLE OF CONTENTS

ACKNOWLEDGMENTS

Thank you my family, Brittany, Gabriella and my beautiful wife Jodie. Together you provided the encouragement and motivation that allowed me to pursue my passions in life.

Special thanks to Dr. Matt James and The Empowerment Partnership for the training and the learnings of the mind through NLP.

Cover: The Thinker by Auguste Rodin

Editing by Daphne Parsekian

CHAPTER 1

YOUR MINDSET

The Operating Manual Is Not the Training

If you find this statement too abstract, perhaps another way of stating this that will make greater sense to you is that the operating manual for your computer is not the computer.

That may sound odd at first, but take a moment to study the statement—that concept—and realize the true meaning and its ramifications. Some of you, especially those with any familiarity with NLP, may have heard it presented as "the map is not the territory."

Stated more simply yet, this means that if you looked at the map of San Francisco, for instance, it would only be a representation of that area on a piece of paper or on your computer screen.

When you are actually physically there, you may personally find it represented to you in an entirely different way than anyone else, including the person standing right next to you at that exact moment in time.

However, while you're there at that exact moment in time, it becomes your reality in every sense!

Where one person may think it's noisy or smelly and crowded with too many people milling about, you may think it is lively, active, and inspiring.

The same example can be used to associate a restaurant or dining experience you may have had. Perhaps you have recommended a restaurant to someone who later told you that it was awful and complained about nearly everything in such a way as to leave you feeling bewildered because their description does not remotely match your experience—your reality.

In your internal representation of the experience, the modest décor, friendly waiters, and well-prepared food were a good value for your money, while the other diner saw the décor as gaudy or crude and the food as being ordinary or maybe even ill-prepared.

Their internal map of their world was different than your map.

It didn't change the restaurant or what you found enjoyable about it, because it was your representation and experience. It was in every sense your reality and no one else's. That's what matters, and that's what you need to master in order become a better communicator with yourself and others.

Why your passage to wealth, prosperity, and fulfillment relies so heavily on this concept is because the way that we think things are, the model of our world, is not necessarily completely accurate.

What's important to recognize and realize is that what we've got in our heads—in our minds—is not absolutely true and accurate. This is where so many of our problems actually lie—not just in our pursuit and understanding of wealth but in everything we do and experience in life.

All of us have a version of the world that we've spent some time developing, understanding, and accepting so that we have a reference point to make sense of things. The trouble is as soon as we start to buy into and accept this version of reality, we only start to see things that fit in it.

So when we see or experience something that doesn't really fit into it, we tend to discount it. We tell ourselves, "That's not right," or "That's not true." Now that might be an accurate description of what just occurred, but it equally might not be. It could be what we've just seen just doesn't fit with our model of the world.

What we need to do is readjust our model instead of just dismissing or deleting this bit of information as being irrelevant or worthless to us.

We can find this throughout our lives. We see it in bigotry and prejudices, and we see it our finances and our journey toward wealth and fulfillment.

As we progress through life and harbor these limiting beliefs, we reinforce our presuppositions and close ourselves off to solutions and change. We forget that our map is only a map. We start to really believe that the way we are perceiving the world is true and accurate.

The other place we need to watch out for is where the map ends and we say, "There isn't anything more than this; this is all there is." It may very well be that there is far more territory and many more things beyond the confines of our personal map. When we have this mindset, we stop looking, and that includes looking for solutions.

We need to expand our maps and look beyond our self-imposed limitations. Along the way, you will encounter experiences and events and see things that you're absolutely sure can't be correct. Only later on will you discover that you were wrong. This means there is a whole bunch of information and opportunities out there that you will never take advantage of. This should become abundantly clear that this could negatively affect your finances and overall wealth.

When you take a moment to think about everyone you know, you can probably think of someone who has a map that isn't as developed as it should be, maybe a much more simplistic view of the world than it should be. It may be one that doesn't particularly work for them, and you can probably recognize that in other people. The question then becomes, could you recognize that in yourself?

Can we take the time to almost float above our map and ask, "What does this give me, what are the results of seeing the world this way, and what does this do for me?"

Here's the beauty of this process. Anywhere you're in conflict or stuck, or things are different or difficult, there will be some interruption of your map and therefore some need or benefit from enriching that—to understand it!

There is a valuable exercise you can use to make the process easier for you, and it's called second positioning. Here you take someone else's point of view, which causes you to create a new map. You can then say, "What if I saw myself from over here?"

A valuable exercise I use with my clients is to have them imagine themselves floating high above their map. I have them try to give a size and shape and identify any soft edges, maybe a little dull and not as clear or focused as other portions of the map. I have them then imagine it a little larger and more flexible so it can accommodate and integrate new data. We then try to locate where it might overlap with other people's maps as well as where it interferes and conflicts with other people's maps.

We can identify how to make the map bigger and focus on areas to accomplish this mindset. The bigger and more enriched your model, the more you'll be able see new things and interact with new people with a sense of comfort and ease. This results in increased opportunities.

When you change your model and map of the world, it's quite common to question whether the new map is right or wrong. A better, more useful question to ask yourself is, does this new map work for me?

So the key to knowing when you should look at your map or model of the world is when things aren't working and you're seeking a change or solution.

There Is Only Feedback—Never Failure!

You want one, and maybe you even feel you need one. How many times have you felt empowered after you refused or discarded one?

I could go on, but by now you're wondering, what is it that I want? Do I really feel I need one? What am I missing that's so empowering if I don't get it?

The answer is an EXCUSE!

We want an excuse to blame and justify why we did something we shouldn't have, or we want an excuse to keep us from doing something we know we really must.

When we take action and push through and accomplish our task, we no longer want or need an excuse. We've empowered ourselves through our actions, which motivates us even further.

We've broken barriers and worked through limiting beliefs and decisions, and we're free to move on—to advance on our journey toward fulfillment and innovation.

The next time an EXCUSE stares you in the face, recognize it for what it is. Defeat it, and don't be afraid of failure for taking it on.

The great Vince Lombardi once said, "Win without boasting. Lose without excuses." It's about taking responsibility for life and how you choose to live it.

Always remember there is no failure, only feedback.

Understanding and accepting this premise is extremely empowering in all aspects of life and absolutely required on your journey to true wealth.

When you try something and it doesn't work out as expected, many times your initial response is "I've failed," and maybe you even give up.

Depending on the seriousness of the undertaking, you might even end up feeling angry, sad, depressed, guilty, and worried. None of those emotions or feelings serve a useful purpose, and you must realize that no one else shares them; they're yours to own, and they always represent a choice.

Your choice! No one can make you feel them; **you elect to feel the way you do.**

Let's look at some real-life examples in action:

In 1967 the renowned Dr. Christiaan Barnard performed the first human heart transplant, in South Africa. What an awesome responsibility and feat, not only being the first to try such a procedure but clearly one where the outcome involved life or death.

Following the transplant, the recipient of the heart lived for 18 days and died of pneumonia due to the immunosuppressive drugs he was taking. Was the procedure a failure? Should have Dr. Barnard have quit at that point?

Later, another recipient lived for 19 months, and Dr. Barnard went on to perform 10 heart transplants; each time he learned from the previous procedures.

Other surgeons became disappointed in his results, but Dr. Bernard persevered in his efforts. He didn't accept them as failures; he did, however, accept what he learned as feedback!

In each instance, his feedback from every procedure allowed him to learn just enough to allow each successive patient to survive a little longer. No one would ever consider Dr. Barnard a failure.

How about Thomas Edison?

He identified and tried over 1,000 materials while looking for a suitable filament for the lightbulb before he found one that actually worked. The world is a brighter place today as a result.

Where would we be if Edison had decided he was a failure and gave up his passion to bring affordable light to the masses?

How about the talent scout at Decca records that rejected the Beatles as having no future in the music industry and told them so? Did the Beatles say, "Okay, you're right, we gave it our best shot," or did they take the rejection as feedback to move forward?

Lastly, do you remember Trump Airlines? You may not, and you wouldn't be alone. Donald Trump remembers it well and not because it or he failed in the endeavor. Donald doesn't consider his effort to be a failure, because he attributes the effort to lessons learned. He continues to use the feedback to guide him in new ventures.

What would happen if we all learned this message at an early age?

No failures, just feedback!

Part of our evolution to success is recognizing that we see things as they really are and never ever worse than they really are. If you choose to always look at the negative implications and accept them as failures, then you have to be ready to accept and live with a never ending stream of excuses for you to do nothing!

Accept them as feedback, learn and improve in each instance, and soon you will find yourself achieving your dreams and passions in a meaningful and supportive way.

You Didn't Hear a Thing That I Said

Do you often find yourself providing "clear, concise advice or instructions" only to find the exact opposite action was undertaken or worse—no action at all?

How do you react? Do you revisit instructions and advice, or do you let the "failure" of inefficient and expected follow-through distract you from your original intentions, goals, and objectives?

If you find that you have to revisit your advice or instructions, try to seek immediate feedback to confirm an understanding of your intended message of mission or goal.

The affirmation or lack thereof may surprise you and help you realize that your audience not only receives your communication of intentions differently but that those communications have differing meanings and consequences dependent on your audiences' filtering process and perceived role in any desired undertaking.

You know what you meant, but did you take the time to determine if they did?

The authoritative desire to announce a "penalty" or disciplinary action related to a continued disregard of your desired outcome may not be the best motivator, especially if the tasking is related to the overall commercial success of your business interest or to your achieving personal wealth.

Maybe it's related to a personal issue, perhaps involving a "chore" or expectation assigned to your child or children where there is no commercial consequence.

If you can step back and construct or tie compliance to a benefit as opposed to a consequence, you will find a far greater "instilled" desire of understanding to fulfill the anticipated tasking.

Assignment of an emotional benefit to all parties promotes influential action, and everyone wins!

Efficient and effective communication is vitally important to all our lives and can have an amazing, empowering positive influence. Equally, if you don't understand the ramifications of miscommunications, your results can be frustratingly negative.

People will respond to what they think you mean. This may be an accurate or inaccurate interpretation of your intended message— your intentions.

Another way of stating the obvious is that **the meaning of communication is the response we get.** Before you read any further, take a moment and fully weigh the implications and meaning of that statement.

Associate that understanding into your life; give it true meaning for you, and see if you can't recognize times where you experienced a disconnect with someone else, maybe a civil dialogue that devolved into a cruel and hurtful discourse.

Take a moment and think about a time when you were arguing or perhaps complaining about something and noticed that the person you were talking to became cynical and started shouting back at you, even when they may have really recognized that they were the ones that had done something wrong.

Recall when someone nearly ran into you in your car. They made a mistake, but you became angry and subconsciously rationalized that anger in your conscious mind and your then present state.

If you confronted them, maybe they were speaking to you calmly and trying to tell you to calm down. Would you be able to calm down—did you calm down? Would or could their manner and method of communication cause you to respond in an alternative way?

We all need to learn to talk TO people instead of AT them!

Most people never take the time to examine their own verbal or kinesthetic communication skills and end up wondering, "Was it something I said?" Probably, but maybe not. It may have been more the way you said it that affected the outcome.

Word choice matters much more than most people think. For instance, some of the most influential words in English are: *You,*

Guarantee, Love, Health, Results, Money, Proven, New, Easy, Discovery, Must, and Will.

If you're in marketing, you might find that these words have some magical hidden or subconscious influence: *Secrets, Now, Sale, Free, Benefits, Announcing, How, Fast, Yes, and Power.* I'm certain there are more, but these will provide a great indicator for a message stirring others to action.

Want more? Think of using the word "because" when responding to just about anything asked, and you'll find people agreeing with you much more frequently. This is especially true when you're asking someone to observe or comply with your request. The word because is accepted as a justifier tied to an action or request.

If you ask questions of your audience, ask questions that lead them to where you want them to go. This will empower them and keep them feeling in control and that their opinion matters, and all the while they're traveling down your path to a mutually agreeable destination or goal.

If we want people to respond appropriately to what we're saying and our intentions; it requires a constant awareness of other people's responses to what we are telling them to make sure there's a mutual level of understanding.

When there isn't, we need to adjust our communication accordingly rather than assuming they understood what we intended or meant for them to understand.

If You Are Doing Something That Does Not Seem to Work, Stop Doing It, & Do Something Different

For those of us that are following our path to wealth, prosperity, abundance, and fulfillment, this becomes one of the hardest barriers or challenges to recognize and break through.

Typically, it's because we haven't developed the training and awareness to recognize that we're caught in an unproductive cycle.

Think and picture this, but under no circumstances try this at home:

- What would happen if you ran into a concrete wall head first?

- What would happen if you tried it again and again and again?

- What would have to happen for you to learn that concrete walls and your head don't necessarily go well together at any speed?

The reality is that in life, we are each responsible for our own lives, and even though we might not be able to control events around us, **we can always control how we respond to them**.

If we always respond in the same way, then we must expect the same results regardless of how we feel about them.

There is always a solution to every challenge, and the question becomes, are you prepared to keep looking for that solution? **Are you employing your feedback?**

You will never have any trouble finding a reason not to do something; the challenge is to stay positive and find the reasons to do something different. If what you're doing isn't working, try something different.

We've all heard the Will Rogers saying that **"if you find yourself in a hole, quit digging."**

Choice? You Can't Handle a Choice!

Imagine, if you will, absolute fear and terror of ever stepping outside of your home to go shopping, or to school, or maybe even to work. The worst case of anxiety and panic attacks is agoraphobia.

People get to the point where they would prefer to stay in rather than go out into the world. It becomes dangerous for them to go out, and so they become prisoners within their own minds and homes.

This means no holidays, no job, no seeing what is happening outside, except for maybe watching it on TV or through the Internet.

In every instance and throughout our lives, having a choice is always better than having no choice. We only achieve that choice when we develop flexibility and alternative solutions to our challenges.

Far too often when we encounter a problem that seems too

overwhelming, we tend to freeze and do nothing. It's a survival technique; it's in our genes and rests in the most primal regions of our brains.

For those afraid to take a calculated risk and venture outdoors, they become slaves to their homes and the safety of the status quo. As far as they're concerned, all options and choices are cut off; they don't exist.

There is only one way of doing something—only ONE CHOICE to select.

They begin to feel safer indoors and at the same time feel depressed because they're missing out on all life has to offer.

Your financial future and ability to find true wealth is directly tied to your ability to create choices and take reasonable and prudent risks based on those choices.

The Person with the Most Flexibility Can Control the System

Flexibility is about being able to change easily and smoothly with little or no effort.

If we become rigid in our ideas, ideals, and behaviors, we become inflexible and must accept the limiting choices before us. Remember that these are choices we've actually created for ourselves.

It's not that there are no alternatives; it's just that our

representational system—the map of our world—impedes choices unless we can learn to take control of our emotions, our thinking, and ultimately our behavior.

Notice how well you get along with someone when you are flexible in your engagements with them. Flexibility gives you more choices and options and less of an "it's my way or the highway" mindset, outlook, and attitude.

Another example might be a business negotiation where you enter into the process with a set outcome in mind. If you don't achieve that outcome, what are your options, your choices? Have you painted yourself into a corner by being inflexible from the very beginning?

If, on the other hand, you went into the process with a hierarchy of your acceptable outcomes, ones that you've prioritized, you will find you are far more likely to achieve at least one outcome that is acceptable and preferable.

Your flexibility opens up choices, and you are able to present positions or arguments that support your intentioned outcome because you are prepared for any resolution of acceptable outcomes.

Why Did You Do That—You Just Weren't Trying

Even if we are born with some defect, we all have the ability to do the best we can with our existing resources. It's empowering to know, believe, and accept that **everyone is doing the best they can.**

Our behavior is an adaptation of habit and consists of what has worked in the past. The problem or challenge arises when that behavior and our actions no longer produce the intended results.

Do you remember **if you are doing something that does not work, stop doing it, and do something different?**

One of the key challenges is recognizing that every behavior has a positive intention—**as far as the person exhibiting the behavior is concerned.**

It does not mean that the behavior is the best possible choice from a subjective or even objective point of view nor that the behavior has a positive effect or benefits for anyone else. **Far too many do not!**

Both consciously and subconsciously, we as humans strive to make the best decisions we can given what we know and have to work with at the time and in the moment.

Even the most despicable acts and behavior of someone is satisfying their positive intention in the moment. One doesn't have to look too far around them or in the world to find actors engaged in selfishly grotesque and demeaning behavior—but it is still satisfying that actor's positive intention in that moment.

You do not have to accept it, but your empowerment comes from recognizing it.

You Cannot Not Communicate

You meet someone for the first time, and maybe they smile but say nothing. Perhaps they look you up and down, from head to toe, yet no words are spoken. What have they just done, and are they communicating with you?

Most of our language is actually nonverbal. Some studies suggest the number could be as a high as 75% to 90% with only 7% being attributed to the spoken word.

The gestures we use, our postures, and our facial expressions all tell others something. When you realize that your subconscious mind controls your body language, you can see the importance of retraining your mindset and the learnings of your subconscious mind.

We are always communicating even if we think we are not.

How many of you have become frustrated or perhaps upset with a friend, business associate, or family member and decided to give them "the silent treatment"? See, you're communicating even though no words are being spoken.

Frequently missed opportunities are the direct result of miscommunications.

Don't let your ego side-track you from your goals. Learn to become a better communicator within yourself to ensure that you don't fall victim to the dreaded "foot-in-your-mouth" disease. Engage openly and thoughtfully with others, especially those you hold closest to your heart.

Mind, Body, and Spirit Are Indivisible Parts of the Same System

The knowledge that these are indivisible is vital to our success in all aspects of life: to understand that the mind controls the body, the body controls the mind, and our spirit—our higher self or life force—is connected to everything. For instance, you cannot have a feeling without a thought, and then your feelings can produce more thoughts.

In order to achieve to true wealth, prosperity, abundance, and fulfillment, you must develop the right positive attitude or mindset through which you live your life. Healthy minds create healthy bodies, and that helps you achieve your vision and goals while maintaining a state of enjoyment—**the purpose of ecological wealth!**

CHAPTER 2

HOPE & SOLUTIONS THROUGH WELL-DEFINED UNDERSTANDINGS

What is wealth to you? How do you define it? What is wealth's meaning?

One of the most critical elements to your success centers on your ability to identify your *WHY* because it's only after you define and settle on your why that you will be able to determine your *HOW*.

Why are you dissatisfied with your life, your job, your relationships, your wealth? Part of that process involves your ability to define, understand, and become congruent with your true values. If you fall short, even by just a little, you will continue to retain that empty, unsatisfied feeling that presents barriers to solutions and diminishes your hope.

When you think of wealth, are you thinking of money, happiness, health, wellbeing, the ability to provide for others while still living comfortably, doing the things you want to do, and having fun? Or is it just a few of those, maybe none of those?

As you can see, wealth means many things to different people. There's a reason for that, and it may not be one you've ever considered before—until now.

Unfortunately, for many, wealth is nothing more than a number, maybe a "net worth" or a bank account worth a certain dollar figure. "If I only had a million dollars," or "if I only had five million dollars," or "if I only had one hundred million dollars, I would be truly wealthy."

Yes, in that isolated world, if you had five million dollars—you'd have five million dollars! But are you truly wealthy? **That depends on what standards or measures you have decided to define your values of true wealth by!**

If you have "X" amount of money but no one who cares about or loves you and you have no one you love—**are you truly wealthy, or do you JUST have "X" amount of dollars?** What about your health, relationships, and happiness?

We've all heard the phrase "Healthy, Wealthy, and Wise."

Think of it as a three-legged stool. If one or more legs were missing, how stable would the stool really be? Would it be something that you'd be comfortable standing on for years or decades to come?

Sometimes the best lessons can be drawn from real-life scenarios that allow us to imagine or picture what this really means.

Let me tell you about Bill (not his real name); he worked tirelessly at his corporate job and advanced through the ranks, becoming a highly compensated marketing director in a business and career he enjoyed.

He felt that once he reached a target compensation package of $650,000 a year, he would have it made. He and his family would be able to afford the house of their dreams, take family vacations, and generally enjoy what his position and salary would allow.

What Bill discovered, however, was an entirely different outcome than he was expecting. When he reached his "wealthy" goal, he discovered he was far less satisfied than he expected. In fact, he was downright miserable and became depressed and confused.

When he looked back, he realized he had missed two birthdays of two of his children while away on business. He missed countless school plays and an entire season of his oldest son's high school baseball season.

You see, Bill's definition of wealth was essentially nothing more than a dollar figure on his way to his definition of wealth.

Bill discovered that his definition of "wealthy" was nothing like he envisioned it to be and had become depressed and angry at himself which affected all those around him. Bill needed help but wasn't sure where or whom to turn to. Bill had lost all hope.

The good news is Bill learned that there is always HOPE because "wealth" is subjective and that means it is something different to everyone; you need to make it unique to you based on your values and beliefs, not someone else's.

Bill learned that his wealth must be ecological. In order for his quest for wealth to be ecological, he needed to satisfy not only his desires and needs but the desires and needs of those around him. You must ask yourself if it is good for and improves your environment in general.

You must define and accept what true wealth means to you.

The first objective is that **you must understand that you are unique.**

You are unique in every possible way because you and only you have undergone your experiences in the world. No one but you knows what you've seen, heard, smelled, tasted, or felt along life's journey. So how and why is that important to you and your desire to improve or enhance your wealth?

Everything you, and only you, have experienced has created your map, an internal representation of your world. It's the way you perceive, feel, and respond to the various stimuli that bombards you each and every second of the day.

How you internalize and associate that stimuli dictates your response and actions. They can be either empowering or limiting, but either way, **they remain a choice—your choice.**

Your map is different from every other person's map, which means how you perceive your environment and your responses (your behavior) will be different from everyone else's, and it will be limited by your ability to contextualize and express your internal representations.

In fact, so much data comes through your senses on a continuous basis that there's no way for your conscious mind to process it all. Your conscious mind must delete and distort the vast majority of the data or you would become dysfunctional. You would be overwhelmed and overcome by the massive amount of data while trying to sense what's important and what's not, what's dangerous and what's not, and what's beneficial and what's not.

However, your subconscious mind keeps it all even though much is distorted and deleted from conscious memory. When you learn how to access and retrieve that data, you immediately empower yourself with choices and alternatives. **You become flexible—you give yourself choices!**

Those choices create flexibility, and with flexibility, you can create influence and change behavior. You change not only your behavior but your ability to influence others.

Learning the techniques that will allow you to manage your emotional state frees you from having to search for solutions from a negative and miserable state to solving life's challenges from a positive state, a state of empowerment.

YOU and only YOU retain that ability, and it's that ability that will allow you to build a life of wealth, abundance, and prosperity versus building a business or career at the expense of all else, especially your family and the relationships that mean the most to you.

You will recognize that all those "things" that you thought you needed in order to succeed and become "wealthy," no matter how you defined it, are not really necessary.

You already have all the tools and resources required; you just need to be able to create greater personal flexibility and choices allowing you to modify your behavior and take positive action.

Recall the previous section on your map of the world. Learn to recognize and accept your reality, and if it's congruent with your values, you can make a change!

All behavior has structure, and because of that structure, you have the ability to learn, change, and model behavior to produce your desired state for success. This is not always easy—for many, it may never seem easy—but it is always worth the effort.

Earlier you learned that there are positive intentions behind all behaviors, and people make the best decisions for themselves based on what they have at the time. It is important for you to know and accept that if it's right for you...it is right for you! Though it may be right for you, it may not be to others because others do not share your internal map, yet you are satisfying your own internal positive intention.

We all are the product of our intentions. It's our intentions that shape our choices of our vision, beliefs, values, and actions. When you work to achieve your true wealth and prosperity, it's critically important that you master your ability to create flexibility and choice while choosing decisions that are ecological to both you and those around you. If you lose sight of this, you will end up right back where you started or are now.

There are two kinds of intentions: one is conscious, and the other subconscious. Only conscious intentions can produce intended, well-defined outcomes for us. While it is true our subconscious mind also produces outcomes, these are usually not intended outcomes.

Subconscious intentions typically result in bizarre, unproductive behavior and thus poor results. Conscious intentions allow us to be flexible, bending our minds to find solutions toward an objective with a determination to act in a certain way or to do a certain thing to make it happen.

So let's begin.

How do we start to *THINK* in order to understand what our current situation is and make the necessary changes to our behavior that are required to become ecologically wealthy while staying congruent to our values and beliefs?

We start by acknowledging that we don't know what we don't know—at least consciously.

We then employ a "SMART" model to build and satisfy our wealth objectives. We do so consciously and draw upon our subconscious mind to fill in the missing or deleted information.

SMART goals are expressed as *specific, measureable, achievable, realistic, and timed* efforts to achieve well-formed outcomes. The critical difference between results that are likely to be achieved and those that aren't comes down to the crafting of well-formed outcomes.

Having defined what wealth means to you, you are then able to understand and explore "what stops you from…?" Think about that for a moment and realize that the barriers that prevent us from achieving our goals and outcomes are the choices or lack of choices we all create for ourselves.

Here there could be any number of consequences as you explore to find the your "cause." Without the "cause," you can't truly know and embrace the changes necessary to accomplish your well-formed outcome or the "effect."

Understanding this concept is critical to your success because you need to achieve maximum power in your own life in order to direct your outcome. This means **YOU MUST take responsibility for everything that happens in your universe.**

A simpler way of understanding being at cause can be described as an airline pilot flying you from New York to London. If the pilot is not at *cause* and is off by just 1%, the *effect* for you is that you safely land (if you're lucky) somewhere a few thousand miles from your intended destination, such as London.

By exploring and understanding your *cause* and *effect*, you will learn which side of the equation you operate from and how your decisions impact your goals and objectives. You will learn if you live and operate as the **CAUSE** in your life or if **you are the EFFECT of things in your life!**

In order to ground yourself with your *cause*, you need to reconnect with the deleted experiences not represented in your conscious model of the world. You don't recognize that *you really do know what you think you didn't know.* Read that again to make sure you understand the implications and meaning of that statement.

People's lives can always be improved, and with improvement, comes the ecology of your wealth. **Change your perspective and you change your emotions.** Think about how such a change would impact your wealth, prosperity, and fulfillment in life.

If you're depressed, all your solutions come from a state of depression. If you're afraid of taking risks, you will likely never take the actions associated with quality risk in order to improve your circumstances.

A very important factor to creating the wealth you seek is a recognition and acceptance that no other human being can create an emotion in another. You are completely responsible for your own emotions, and with the proper training and coaching, you can learn to accept, reject, or reframe those emotions in such a way that empowers you to positive action.

Once you understand this relationship, you will recognize that the actions of one do not necessarily connect to the actions of another. A simpler way to understand this dynamic is that the act of one did not cause the emotion of another; instead, the emotion was a choice based on your model of your world—and only your world.

Because it is a choice, it can either be a negative influence or a positive and empowering influence. You get to decide, but you must also take responsibility.

Everything is first created in our head, in our mind, as an intention and then in reality. There can be no reality without the intention, whether conscious or subconscious. Think of a house. It cannot become reality until it is created in the mind of the architect then physically constructed.

It comes down to recognizing, accepting, and modifying your attitude, your frame of mind, and your map of reality.

Once you have mastered your self-awareness by answering questions such as the following, it becomes real, meaningful, and achievable:

- **What do I want?**

- **What works?**

- **How do I do that?**

- **What is the difference that truly makes a difference?**

CHAPTER 3

MOTIVATION MOVES YOU FORWARD

So far you've learned that you need to define and refine your definition of wealth, what it means to you, and how it will affect those around you. Finding and defining wealth by keeping it congruent with your values and beliefs, we've learned you can construct your well-defined outcome. You're now inspired and need to put your plan into action.

In order for you to fully take charge, you'll need to find the strength and courage to become your own person. You need to stop allowing others to define who you are and what you're capable of.

Far too often we let our worries and limiting beliefs freeze our actions and create periods of procrastination. These two factors have a disproportionate effect on your ability to not only envision your true ecological wealth but to initiate a positive action plan.

Breaking down your limiting beliefs.

Beliefs make up your world. Whether you think you're right or wrong, you're right! This means that no matter what you believe in your life, it's true for you.

Why is this so important?

It's because if you held the belief that you weren't good enough, you'd probably see the world as a place where you just can't seem to win or succeed.

This might relate to your ideal partner, or about trying to get a job, or your beliefs about money and the ability to earn money or not earn money. Maybe you even feel that money is a bad thing; perhaps you are of the belief that money is bad, the root of all evil, and that it's hard to come by or to achieve the financial success that you want.

There are two things that keep you from achieving the success you seek in life. The first is an emotion, and typically one of "fear," while the second is a limiting belief itself. Usually if you can let go of your limiting belief, you can resolve to do away with the "fear."

Worrying creates more worrying. The more you worry, the more stress is created. This can lead to self-destructive behavior, from everything to nail biting to headaches to insomnia. It most certainly leads to procrastination.

When you allow worry to take over, it can become impossible to regain control over your thoughts and thinking. Worrying is a learned behavior. If you grew up in an environment where it was highly unpredictable as a child, you very likely grew up and developed this habit and have carried it with you throughout your adulthood. It is quite common for someone who was raised by a parent or guardian that worried to model that behavior because that is how we all learned.

The good news is that it is possible to reframe and teach your mind to become more relaxed and controlled, eliminating these barriers to your success.

Now you may be thinking to yourself, if it's so easy, I'll just think about something else. Nice try, but it doesn't work that way...not exactly. The reason it doesn't is because your subconscious mind is driving your ship of life; it's running your belief system.

So how do our beliefs come about? They are a result of or the sum of all our experiences. The things that we've gone through in life up to this moment make us what we are today, at the precise moment you are reading this sentence.

Our experiences include both wonderful times and traumatic times, and when we have a certain number of negative events, they begin to collate into a limiting belief system. The same is true for pleasant or positive experiences as well.

Because this book is about helping you discover, build, and achieve wealth, prosperity, and abundance, let's examine this further in the context of work and a job interview so this concept makes more sense.

Let's say sometime in the past you were going for a job interview and you didn't get it. So you decided to go for another job, and you didn't get that one either. Soon, when you're going for your job interviews, you start to get anxious and nervous. You become confident that you don't know what to say or how to say it, which leads to greater and greater frustration and anxiety.

Soon you begin to think about what the interviewer thinks about you, and this too magnifies your fears about performing well in a job interview.

When we go through a negative experience, our mind can spiral out of control sometimes, and it becomes quite hard to regain control and composure. Soon your body starts to associate negative feelings and beliefs with all interviews and creates a belief that you will never get the job you wanted.

If you're someone who is impacted by worrying, I want to give you this simple five-minute exercise that can help you solve and find your solutions. If you need 15 minutes, that's okay!

First, I want you to take a piece of paper and write down all of the issues that are causing you worry in your life. It doesn't need to be limited to financial matters; it could be issues at your job, family, school, health, past memories, etc.

The key here is to physically make a list—to get it out of your mind and onto the paper.

The next step is to write down solutions to each of these concerns. After you've done this, I want you ask yourself these following questions:

1. **What resources do I require to fix, heal, or improve this issue?**

2. **What resources do I already have that will help?**

3. **Can I do this on my own, or do I need the help of others?**

4. **Do I need to seek professional guidance?**

Next set a goal date for when you want each concern or fix to be solved by. Write down all of the action steps you're going to take to ensure that all of these concerns are solved by the goal date. Make the date realistic as you don't want to reflect on your efforts and become discouraged because you set unrealistic expectations for yourself.

Put the paper away in a safe location, and affirm to yourself that you've spent enough time on the issue for that day AND that you will only think of them again in your next worry session.

Now clear your mind and relax!

By creating a specified time to worry, you're taking back control of yourself. By thinking of solutions, writing them down, setting a goal date, and then taking positive actions toward solutions or fixes, you're making them all much easier to handle.

Sometime things don't seem so troublesome or worrisome when you write them down.

Do this each day for a week and see how you feel. Like anything, it might take some practice, but it works if you stick to it.

Make sure you write down anything you've accomplished as well as any new concerns. Also think of any new actions you can take to complete the list on time.

Remember how we just learned that worry can become a function of modeled behavior? Well, modeled behavior can also become your map to exceptional results just as easily. The best way to change your life is to find people who've already achieved what you seek and then model their behavior.

Unfortunately, we learn and accept bad habits, behaviors, and beliefs along the way that require fixing, and we allow them to limit our potential. Throughout life, your parents, siblings, teachers, friends, authority figures, and others that you communicate with judge you by your age, social standing, education, economic class, religion, gender, sexual orientation, etc.

Some of these judgments or opinions could be positive, like the fact that you're smart, you're a good student, or you're successful. Still others might be negative, like you're not good enough or you're not smart enough, beautiful enough, etc. These judgments and words start to affect your thinking if you accept them as true. When these get reinforced over time, they can program your subconscious mind about beliefs and opinions about yourself.

At our core, we are all sensitive about ourselves. When others say hurtful or negative things about us, we tend to absorb them like a sponge. It's easy to pick up others' negatively charged garbage and carry it with us through life.

It's also not necessarily just words that are spoken to you either. There are also gestures and body movement (body language) that tend to be the window for what others are thinking and feeling about us. Our unconscious mind can pick up on those subtle meanings by the way others carry themselves.

Even if the lips lie, the body always tells the truth because the subconscious mind is controlling those subtle movements and gestures.

If you get a sense that someone or a particular group views you in a negative way, this can also lead to negative self-belief. This all adds up to an image of our self-perception, or all that we believe to be true about ourselves.

You begin to believe all the labels that were placed upon you. These negative beliefs can move you away from your personal power. But once you regain control and are able to move away from the negativity, you can create a new life for yourself and others.

New possibilities emerge and take shape. **Words have the power to harm or to heal.** When others used words to harm us, it becomes all about finding the right words to heal and empower us to change our beliefs. Don't waste too much time on theirs, because their perception is a reflection of their internal representations.

The first step is to become aware of the undesirable self-system that you carry around with you on a daily basis. You may have a lot of wonderful, positive beliefs about yourself, but chances are you have at least one negative self-belief that is holding you back in your life.

Here is how you can regain control and identify and change your limiting beliefs.

Again, we start with a piece of paper, and you write what you believe to be true about yourself in two columns: one for the positive, and one for the negative.

Looking at each self-belief, I want you to write down how each one makes you feel. Then become aware of how each one of these beliefs affects your life and those around you.

Then ask yourself, "Who would I be and what could I be without each of these negative beliefs?"

I then want you to think about the times when and places where the negatives are not true. Then write out self-affirmations that you can give yourself that will replace the negative self-beliefs.

Did you discover the words that will heal the hurt? I am good enough, I am smart, I am kind, etc. Repeat them out loud whenever you need to give yourself some inner strength.

We all have the resources to make these changes within ourselves, and when you decide to make the changes, you can learn from these occasions **because it's all a matter of choice.** You can take all the negative self-beliefs and file them under garbage.

Change your power, create your own boundaries, and stop waiting for others to prove themselves trustworthy, supportive, and safe.

You decide how those relationships are going to be defined. This empowers you to stop waiting on others; you create your own circumstances for success and prosperity, because if you don't, no one else will.

There are those that will espouse all you really have to do is create and maintain the practice of positive thinking in order to discover your true wealth and prosperity. Positive thinking is important for many reasons; however, prosperous thinking is a greater call to action.

Why is this important for you individually?

We only have to look up the definition of prosperous to find the answers. The *Merriam-Webster* dictionary defines prosperous as auspicious and favorable; marked by success or economic wellbeing and enjoying vigorous and healthy growth.

Does this not define and capture your true desires to become wealthy in a holistic and ecological way? **To truly satisfy your desires and needs as well as the desires of those around you while improving your environment in general.**

By becoming a better communicator with yourself and others, you learn to unlock your mind and thinking in order to create better health, increased financial success, a happier personal life, an increased level of personal education, and a deeper spiritual life, no matter how you elect to define what spiritual means to you.

Once you've decided to improve and master your own internal communications, you will develop a better and deeper understanding of your values and how those values drive your motivation.

This understanding profoundly affects how you feel after you've accomplished a goal or met an objective in your journey and passage toward empowerment, wealth, and prosperity.

Your vision and goals must be clear and compelling and must connect to your true values in order to have a satisfying meaning. Your vision must encompass your positive future and not include what you're afraid of.

Your values also differ across the six basic areas of life. You will have a set of meaningful values related to your career, your spirituality, your health and fitness, and your relationships to family and others along with your personal growth and development.

How you decide to assess, live with, and integrate those values will determine the magnitude of your success and wealth. Again, it's not and has never been a matter of dollars and cents that measures your level of success, wealth, and prosperity.

By achieving a higher level of understanding of your values, you will be in a position to decide if you need to move away from or toward beliefs and empowering decisions in your life.

Do you move toward or away from conflict, risk, wealth, or poverty?

The process allows you to challenge and develop your focus because you tend to get what you focus on—even if it's the negative. But here you will learn to focus on what you want—the positive. This is why is very important that you always focus toward what you want to achieve and not on the results you don't want.

Focusing on the results you don't want causes you to subconsciously focus on the negative.

CHAPTER 4

YOUR TRANSFORMATION

What's Your Potential?

A lot of people go through life with the feeling that they are stuck. No matter what they do or how hard they try, for some reason it just never seems to be enough.

Then again, a great number of people seem to have found the secret, and no matter what they do, it always seems to be just right, and everything works out according to plan.

The degree of difference between the two might surprise you. Successful people have learned to look within themselves, to become successful dreamers, and to take advantage of their *discovery moments*.

What are *discovery moments*? These are when you learn about yourself and you discover that your life does not have to be determined by how bad things are but rather by how great your potential is.

Successful business people and athletes learn to tell and convince themselves: *"I'M GOING TO MAKE IT NO MATTER WHAT!"* They get up every day, and that's the first thing they do. They reinforce their state of certainty that nothing is going to get in their way.

They've learned to build themselves to a peak state. They feel it; they anchor it so they can revisit and reconstruct it whenever it's needed.

It's best exemplified in athletes because that's where it's most noticeable. When a top performing athlete has an off day, they don't look to external conditions for excuses. They look within themselves and try to identify the small, incremental changes that need to be made in order to improve.

It's their ability to self-examine and not blame the external forces of their environment, and to identify those small and subtle changes, which, when practiced and improved upon, become remarkable achievements in success.

You seldom hear a top athlete blame a performance on the weather, the track, the lighting, etc., because they know everyone else competing against them endured these same conditions. Blaming an external source creates limiting beliefs that are difficult to overcome until you learn to recognize and accept your *discovery moments*.

Next time you're watching a sporting event, look for routines: the batter that adjusts the straps on his glove before each pitch, the swimmer that claps their hands before getting ready on the blocks, and the golfer that twirls his club or approaches his golf ball as if the ball might attack him at any moment.

They are putting themselves in a state of certainty and visualizing the task or race before them. They are building upon all the small, incremental changes they discovered, bringing all of them to bear in that particular moment.

So what's your potential?

We all have the power of choice—the choice to choose what we focus on, the meanings of our actions or inactions, and what to do as a result. It comes down to the *decisions* of our lives, not the *conditions* of our lives. Pay attention and look for your *discovery moments*, find your potential, embrace it, and share it with others.

We must start by defining our inner values, learning and truly understanding ourselves. This develops a greater understanding of our abilities and limitations in communicating not only with ourselves but with others.

By upgrading your ability to communicate with yourself and thereby others, you will develop the ability to say it the way you want to.

The manner in which you state your goals and objectives makes a difference. A goal stated positively is much more accomplishable than one stated negatively.

Don't believe me? Look at these two statements of intention.

1. I would like to lose some weight, but I can't seem to break the _____ pound mark.

2. I will become healthier and enjoy my tapered look and newfound energy when I lose ___ pounds.

You may be thinking "How?" or "Can I get rid of a negative emotion or belief?" in order to allow yourself to move forward. You do it all the time; you just do not realize it consciously.

For example, maybe you used to be afraid of the dark and now you're not. This means that already at some level you know how to let go of a negative emotion.

It's vitally important to your success that you develop a desire and ability to manage your transformation. In today's world of information overload involving text messages, tweets, phone calls, emails, etc., you will need to keep a clear head and be able to focus.

By allowing these distractions, you create walls or barriers that end up blocking your ability to take decisive action. This results in keeping you from becoming productive even though you may feel like you're accomplishing quite a lot.

Once you've defined your innermost values, you'll be able to define your purpose. This will help you with your focus on the short-term in order to achieve your long-term vision, goals, and objectives.

Becoming wealthy and prosperous and achieving abundance in your life requires discipline and **the ability to reject certain opportunities when they present themselves.** This requires you to develop the ability to not only say "NO" more often but to be able to do so in such a way that you don't dwell on or develop any regrets during the process.

Those that achieve true wealth do so by not trying to do everything and be everything to everyone. Trying to do everything causes you to end up being confused and unfocused. **By learning to say no to heightened opportunities, you create the ability and opportunity to say "YES" to the greatest opportunities.**

This may be something on sale, a "hot" stock tip or investment offering, or anything else in life that presents and distracts from your SMART goals for a well-defined outcome.

Most have a problem with productive priorities because they fail to create a viable plan associated with their vision. **By having too many "number one" priorities, you become overly reactive instead of being proactively driven toward your vision of prosperity.**

We've already learned that change for many is a process of habit and is necessary in order achieve desired results. You may be familiar with the quote of Anthony (Tony) Robbins: **"If you do what you've always done, you'll get what you've always gotten."**

Or perhaps you've heard Albert Einstein's brilliant observation: **"Insanity is doing the same thing over and over again and expecting different results."**

When we question outcomes yet make a decision based on the premise of **"that's the way we've always done it,"** we are often setting ourselves up for disastrous and disappointing results. **Building true wealth, prosperity, and abundance typically involves some level of smart, strategic risk taking or action.**

Frequently, this also includes investing in various financial markets. If you were to take all your liquid assets, dig a big hole, then bury them in your backyard, you would not be taking a smart, strategic risk or action. I'm not remotely familiar with the "bury all the assets in the yard" allocation model, and neither should you be.

Because of emotion and a failure to control your state leading to logical decisions instead of limiting decisions, people tend to buy something that maybe runs up in value for a brief or even an extended period of time, and they fall in love with it no matter what.

CHAPTER 5

TRADITIONAL INVESTING & WEALTH BUILDING

Here we take a look at "traditional" investment advice and wisdom in an effort to examine why it's so important for you to align your financial goals and objectives with your true values and desired outcomes.

We know that our efforts to accumulate true *wealth* is unique to each of us, and we've learned that in order for us to enjoy *prosperity* and *fulfillment,* we always make sure we remain ecological in our desired outcome—that our efforts are in line with our true values and that they satisfy not only our needs but the holistic needs of those we're closest to.

We do this for many reasons; one of the most critical ones is to ensure a degree of certainty that we can care for ourselves and our loved ones, not only throughout life but at the end of life and beyond—so that we can enjoy a life of *wealth, prosperity*, and *abundance.*

When we invest in the capital markets, it's easy to get hung up on benchmarking our performance to those of tradition or typical indexes, like the S&P 500 or the Russell 2000. The problem that this creates for you is a sense of excitement when you out-perform or a sense of dissatisfaction when you under-perform.

What all of the indexes have in common is absolutely no sense of what's right for you! They fail to take into account what your risk tolerance is, your time horizons, and your specific goals and objectives. Yet we as investors continually measure our outcomes against these benchmarks.

When looking to these benchmarks, always keep in mind that past performance is not an indicator of future performance. If your time frame is 35 years before you're even considering retiring, why would you care what the S&P 500 did last week or last year?

When we allow ourselves to get caught up in the comparison trap, we tend to lose sight of our intended outcome. The establishment of that intended outcome far outweighs any performance metric.

Think of your investment outcome like a trip across the country by car. Would you just start driving without a plan, a map, or a GPS system of some sort? You could well find yourself driving in circles.

Like investing for your retirement, if you know you have a certain value of fixed expenses that will be due each and every month or year, you can't afford to continually drive in circles, especially if you have a fixed amount of time in order to get from one coast to the other.

In retirement, you will still require money and income. They are not one and the same! In retirement, you could run out of money, but as long as you're still above ground, you will still require income.

You will have fixed costs associated with property taxes if you own a home, paid for or not. You will probably want to eat once in a while. You may even require a doctor's care. All of these require income to sustain you or your loved ones in later life.

With early and proper planning, all of these concerns can be accounted for with some degree of certainty. For those of you that do not use the services of a financial professional, the responsibility rests squarely on your shoulders to take and make reasonable decisions based on calculated risks. You have learned that your limiting beliefs can and do negatively impact your ability to make decisions.

We begin by looking at "retirement savings" and our ability to sustain our lifestyle after our working or productive years. As we approach retirement age, it is helpful to know that as a general rule, your portfolio will produce a higher withdrawal rate when the market has a low price to earnings (P/E) ratio—a tool that can be used to estimate the future long-term returns (15+ year cycles) of the stock market. (It doesn't work very well in predicting short-term market returns.)

If you're a retiree, it can be used to establish a good starting withdrawal rate, an amount that could safely be withdrawn each year with the ability for subsequent years' withdrawals to increase with inflation.

Many of you may be familiar with the 4% drawdown mantra, where you can theoretically sustain a withdrawal rate of 4% without outliving your principal. But let's research this further.

There was a very interesting study presented in the *Journal of Financial Planning* in October of 1994 by Bill Bengen CFP® (he is widely referenced in multiple studies for his work on this topic), in which he made some observations that remain valid today when calculating withdrawal rates in the context of rolling, 30-year timeframes, a timeframe which could be considered reasonable for a retiree at or near 62. Among his observations were:

- When the price to earnings ratio of the stock market (S&P 500) is below 12, safe withdrawal rates range from 5.7% to 10.6%.

- When the stock market's price to earnings ratio is in the range of 12–20, safe withdrawal rates range from 4.8% to 8.3%.

- When the price to earnings ratio of the stock market is above 20, safe withdrawal rates range from 4.4% to 6.1%.

Then, in 2012, Bill Bengen again made news by proclaiming he wasn't convinced the rule still applied given our current economic environment.

When Bengen first recommended the 4% drawdown in the 1994 *Journal of Financial Planning* article, it was based on a "worst case" scenario of an investor that retired in 1969.

This is critical to the assumptions and advice some financial professionals and do-it-yourselfers relied on for decades. These assumptions were built on the concept of a balanced portfolio, where it was typically allocated between roughly 60% equities and 40% fixed income to a 50/50 portfolio.

Much of the problem associated with his thesis were the limitations of reconstructing historical retirees' portfolios from 1926 forward, trying to capture asset class returns and inflation to model safe withdrawal rate projections.

Bengen completed his work in 1993, when there were 38 complete 30-year retirement periods available to study (1926–1963). Today there are 58 from 1926 to 2012, although at the time, there were only 57 from 1926 to 1982.

His updated studies concluded that the retiree that retired on January 1, 1969, was the "big loser." The conclusion determined that the sequence of investment returns is crucial for portfolio longevity. This is a prime reason financial planning can be so critical. The time to determine you're going to run out of money is not when you run out money!

Over the past few years, the availability and use of financial calculators have proliferated on the Internet. The unfortunate part of most of these calculators are that they either force you to make unrealistic assumptions or, in some cases, assign those assumptions for you by default. These calculators can be helpful for transition points to help you understand and make those transitions, but let's explore more closely why you should be very careful when relying on these outputs.

If you're looking for that magic number that says "you've made it, go out and play, enjoy the rest of your life, you have nothing to worry about," it doesn't exist. Consider the variables of input and you'll understand what I'm talking about.

Start with the inflation rate and how it affects your investment returns. The amount of money you make off your assets is only what your nominal return is minus the inflation rate. In addition, it also affects your expenses over time, so it works against you on both sides of the equation.

Did you know in 2012 it took $6.47 to buy what $1 in 1969 would buy?

You must therefore be able to identify your **personal inflation rate**, which is driven by your lifestyle.

The official rate of inflation is really a political issue, and it taxes savers and those with assets. It's essentially a mechanism used by the government for redistributing money that you thought you saved. Therefore trying to predict the future inflation rate is like trying to predict the political future.

Because of this, we have a problem with the first variable of trying to assess future values and needs. There are PhDs that spend their entire careers trying to predict inflation rates one year into the future, but with these calculators, **you're expected to predict it 25 to 40 or more years in the future?**

If you get just the one assumption wrong by a couple of percentage points (which is very easy to do), you could have twice as much as you need in retirement assets than you originally forecasted, or you could have only half as much as you need to get by.

Let's go back to the driving coast to coast example. A good way to think about this is to envision driving from the east coast to the west and trying to predict the exact minute of arrival. Along the way, you'll need additional data and instruments, like a gas gauge, a map, or a GPS to make sure you're even headed in the right direction.

Next we need to look at investment returns. Typically, many rely on the "average" market returns, and that number is typically based on the past 70 years of market data to calculate growth going forward. There are at least three problems with relying on that assumption.

The first one is the assumption that we're in the midpoint of that market cycle so we can expect the same average going forward for the second half, when in fact the market may well be overvalued and unable to sustain that rate of return going forward. The second is failing to account for market volatility and the sequence of returns (the magnitude of returns over any extended period of time). The third is the index against which performance expectations are actually measured.

Valuation is statistically relevant to your expected return over a 10- to 15-year time horizon. That time frame is very relevant to retirement planning and your ability to create and sustain any level of meaningful wealth.

So when you look to valuation, you should try to determine where you are in the market cycle as markets tend to move from overvalued to undervalued and back to overvalued over extended periods of time. These calculations affect the mathematical expectancy of your portfolio.

Market cycles alone do not account for volatility, which can have a profound effect on your portfolio's valuation, especially if you've begun the drawdown phase where you're taking money out for living expenses. As you draw down your portfolio, you dramatically affect the ability to produce that "average return" in order to predict long-term retirement cash flow needs.

Risk management is a key tenant to retirement portfolio management. If you were a retiree who retired in 2000 and lived through the roughly 50% decline of the market and were counting on the 4% withdrawal rate to meet long-term expenses, you would have knocked out 60–70% of your assets without even adjusting for volatility, just off spending alone. The probability of ruin in retirement is highly correlated to the sequence of returns in the first 10–15 years.

The next vital piece of data in order to predict whether your portfolio will sustain you through your retirement is your life expectancy. Go ahead; try to nail that one in advance. Even if you are confident in picking a number, are you going to plan to go broke on your 95th birthday? What if you die at 75 and there's this huge portfolio you were never able to take advantage of?

With the advances of healthcare, there may be every reason to believe that if you're reasonably healthy now, you could live into your 100s. There is no statistical reality for any single lifespan, and who wants to be "average" when it comes to forecasting your "end-date."

What if you work an extra 10 years in a job that you hate? Is that a guaranteed loss as you've lost 10 years of life doing something you really didn't want to do in the first place? Remember, everything we do in life involves *choice*—including the choice to stay at or in a career that makes you miserable, regardless of compensation.

Planning for retirement is not an easy process, and it requires flexibility and the ability to adapt to life's choices and economic realities.

If you're inclined to use simple online calculators, remember to carefully calculate the effect of your input data and change the data both up and down to see how it affects your long-term prospects.

The only real data input that you can control is your lifestyle choices. You may have limited control over the length of time you elect to work, especially if self-employed, but the savings rate and rate of expenditures are the most malleable under your control.

As you can see, there are many variables to consider when planning for your retirement and even after you enter your retirement years. The process is not one of "set it and forget it" but one that you should regularly revisit, especially if you have a significant, life-changing event occur.

For those of you that conduct your own portfolio management, you probably already know that successful investing is hard but that it doesn't necessarily require genius.

While this book is not meant to be a treatise on investing, a certain level of investing knowledge and understanding is generally required in order to achieve a life of fulfillment, abundance, wealth, and prosperity.

So for those reasons, it's important to spend some time addressing how your ability to communicate with and within yourself is critical to your journey and passage to achieving your vision and goals.

Read this statement very carefully: *Your investments don't care, and they don't know you or love you or anything else.* They have no memory of what you paid, where they've been, or where they may end up.

Those that tend to fall "in love" with a particular security or investment may even buy more as the trends, fundamentals, or markets roll over and retrace, stealing from them all the gains they failed to lock in before ultimately falling below—sometimes well below—their entry price.

You may think and truly believe "I know it's coming back. I can feel it; it has been too good to me in the past. I'll just buy some more, and when it does come back, I'll be that much further ahead."

If you owned an investment that was worth $1,000 and it fell 50% in value, your investment would have lost $500 and be worth $500. You may be thinking, "Well, I need to make back the 50% to get back to where I was before the price dropped." Not true!

If your investment went back up by 50%, it would be worth $750, not the original $1,000 before the drawdown. You will need to make a 100% return on your money just to get back to where you started.

If you fall into this category, you have a limiting belief that is resulting in a limiting decision, which can and will only end badly over the long term.

Sure, sometimes securities do come back and go on to higher

valuations, and when you're on that ride, it's a great feeling. But if you don't have some sense of what to look for in evaluating both fundamentals and technical indicators, you're basing your investment future and outcome on little more than hopes, dreams, and emotions being controlled subconsciously by your limiting beliefs.

Besides determining where, from a performance standpoint, you decide to exit your "relationship," you need to also be sure you haven't risked your financial future on this "ungrateful" and "uncaring" affiliation.

Investing is not unlike a lot of other things in life. You need to control what you can control. Remember, you cannot control the price movement of a security or trade, but you can control your emotional state, your entry price, your selling price, and your position size.

Warren Buffett, the "Oracle of Omaha," once remarked that "Success in investing doesn't correlate with I.Q. once you're above the level of 25. Once you have ordinary intelligence, what you need is the temperament to control the urges that get other people into trouble in investing."

This is the same as stating "You must be able to control your state and emotions to avoid getting into trouble when investing."

Most people don't take the time to consider why they really make investment decisions. Reasons can be as diverse and disparate as getting that hot tip from a friend, from listening to the talking heads on the radio or TV, or from reading an article about the stock you need to buy and hold for the next ten years.

In reality, there are motivators that are running in the background, and they can seriously impact how, what, and when you tend to make these decisions. Let's explore some of these further.

There is the recency effect or "recency bias," where we tend to remember those things that happened most recently in time. We also tend to have a "confirmation bias," where there are certain things we just want to believe are true. It wasn't all that long ago when the "recency bias" was that real estate always goes up and never falls in value (we all know how that played out).

Complicating the matter is that we are inclined to seek out information that tends to reinforce our studies or match our beliefs and opinions. We actively seek out and look for confirmation because it reinforces our beliefs.

One of the best examples to demonstrate this concept might be a real estate purchase. When you're looking to buy the house, you tend to look for reasons why it's financially sound over the long term.

You might cite the usual positive aspects of the purchase, including your consideration of it as an asset that is likely to appreciate over the long term and that you'll receive a small tax break related to paying the mortgage interest.

However, many buyers likely ignore the fact that they're likely to move out of the house before aggregate equity gains outweigh the financial advantage achieved over renting.

I'm not suggesting you should always consider renting over buying, but when we build true ecological wealth, it's important to identify and weigh as many variables as possible. **This is called financial planning!**

Then there's the prospect of losing money and the effect and influence this causes on our behavior. The brain typically reacts to losing money the same way as it does to pain, which is something we try to avoid if at all possible.

In the investing world, that's not always possible, and producing decisions that are more likely to side with gains over losses is not always easy. In fact, studies have demonstrated that when presented with an even chance of winning $150 or losing $100, we tend not to take the chance for the 50% additional gain. People tend to reject a risk where their possibility of winning is anything less than twice the amount of the possible loss.

Financial professionals seek to recognize this relationship through some of the questions presented to you in order to allow the adviser to appropriately assess your investment tendencies and level of acceptable risk tolerance.

It is the fear of losing money and experiencing the associated pain that keeps most of us from taking on risk, even strategic, acceptable levels of risk. Many investors today have parked their funds in bank CD and money market funds paying an inflation adjusted negative real rate of return. **They'd rather have the return of their money instead of a return on their money.**

Unfortunately, with the return of their money, they can no longer purchase what they could have with those nominal dollars due to inflation.

Loss aversion sometimes commands the investor's attention whereby they tend to focus on the one investment that's losing money even though their portfolio as a whole is doing well. Sadly, many investors are more than willing to sell winners to take some profits but at the same time struggle to accept defeat in the case of losers.

It is the fear of regret that tends to paralyze the investor when dealing with loss aversion. Such tendencies preclude our ability to distinguish between a bad investment decision and a bad investment outcome. Another way of looking at this is through "selective memory." Instead of remembering the past accurately, we tend to remember it selectively so that it suits our needs.

Another type of *selective memory* is known as "representativeness," which is, in effect, a mental shortcut that causes us to give too much weight to recent evidence and events and not enough from the more distant past.

Many investors can become overconfident when they drink their own Kool-Aid and believe their boundless ability as a human makes them smarter than they really are. In fact, some studies have shown an interesting side of this when people say they were 90% sure of something then studies showed they were only right 70% of the time.

This confidence is not always a bad thing; however, overconfidence can hurt an investor when they believe they know more than the person on the other side of their trade.

Self-handicapping could be considered the opposite of overconfidence, where we try to explain any possible future poor performance with a rationale that may or may not be true. In everyday life, you might see this in your child or yourself, where they or you say you're not feeling well just before a big presentation. This is done so if the presentation doesn't go well, we'll have an explanation as to why. We are creating the *effect* to justify the *cause*.

People typically give too much weight to their recent investment experiences, where they extrapolate trends that are at odds with long-term averages and statistical tendencies. Investors tend to be more optimistic when markets are going up and pessimistic when they're going down.

We often see order where it doesn't exist and interpret success as the result of our unique skillsets. Also, we tend to be overconfident in our own ability, and investors and investment analysts tend to be particularly overconfident in areas where they have some knowledge and experience, but they let emotions drive their decisions.

Many of you may have experienced a nice night at dinner where you're looking at the wine list trying to decide on what bottle to buy. You avoid the $250 bottle as being too expensive and settle on the $50 bottle for the table.

You might be surprised to learn that frequently the restaurant doesn't even carry the $250 bottle, or if they do, they might have just one on reserve. Its sole presence on the menu is to drive you to the "previously" expensive selection that <u>wasn't selling</u> as well as expected until the restaurant <u>raised</u> the price by presenting you with a choice they knew would trigger a predictable psychological response.

Don't feel deceived or cheated. If you enjoyed the bottle, then it was the right decision for you. You bought the $50 bottle, it was great, the dinner was great, and you felt better for avoiding the $250 decision.

You see, we're not all that unpredictable after all.

In reality, there are motivators that are running in the background, and they can seriously impact how, what, and when you tend to make these decisions, like the prospect of losing money. Unfortunately, it is well documented that many investors use the "recency bias" when reviewing their quarterly statements to make investment decisions based on negative short results and then miss the market's rebound.

All things being equal, remember, if you're trading anything other than an open-ended mutual fund with the ability to generate additional shares for purchase, the security you're buying because you "know" it is about go up was acquired from a counter-party that sold it because they "knew" it was about to go down.

"I'm sorry. It won't happen again. I'll be better, I'll get better, I promise. Please don't leave me!"

No, this is not a conversation between you and a friend or your significant other. This is your investment that you knew you should have left long ago, but maybe, just maybe, it would come back, improve, and get better, so you hang on.

Do you remember Enron, or WorldCom, or a hundred other companies that went from stellar performance to non-existence?

Briefly, for those of you that aren't familiar with a "trailing stop," it is a defined percentage away from a securities current market price, and it goes up as your security rises.

As the trailing stop rises, it will never go back down; it stays the fixed percentage below the highest level attained by your security even if your position trends sideways or starts to lose value. There are many ways to use trailing stops, and you can even adjust them to account for dividend distributions.

When it comes to your financial wealth and your satisfaction that you're doing the right thing and have your decision making process under control, remember that if one part of your life is completely out of control, eventually it will impact ever other area of your life, even those which you are extremely good at.

This is why balance is important and why you have to constantly work on every part of your life, not just the one focused only on your career. Working hard is important, but just as important is taking time for your family and for yourself beyond the work. If you don't, eventually it will catch up to you and hurt the very thing you are truly better at than anyone else.

It is true that many of us tend to focus only on the short-term view and lose sight of the long-term ramifications from our actions and behaviors.

We must always keep the big, long-term future in focus as well as the present to make sure we make the best decisions possible both for the short and long term. A focus only on the short term without the long term also in view will lead you astray and jeopardize your ability to reach your goals and desired outcomes.

We must learn to surround ourselves with people who challenge us and make us better than we thought we could be rather than those who just travel with us on the wrong road, making the same decisions over and over again.

If you truthfully examine your own life and career, you may find that many of you fight constantly with your egos and that your ego is more in control over your portfolio and strategies than even you care to admit.

I know also that far too many of us waste a lot of time focusing on the external elements around us (brokers, gurus, strategies) instead of working on the internal (our emotions, our egos), which you have now learned has much more of an influence on our ultimate success.

In addition, we all have the habit of blaming everyone else for the mistakes we have made, whether it's the Fed, the markets, brokers, gurus, program trading, our spouses, Wall Street, and so on. These are the ramifications of your internal representational system and reflect limiting beliefs that lead to limiting decisions.

You can break the cycle, but it requires you becoming more aware and more in tune with yourself and acquiring the ability to recognize the true intentions of others. You must learn to fine-tune your own internal communications so that you can adequately assess the feedback you receive from others.

Hopefully we can learn from the mistakes of others so we can avoid making them on our own, or at least be able to recognize it when we do make the same mistakes so that we can stop them from taking control before it is too late.

CHAPTER 6

WEALTH, PROSPERITY & FULFILLMENT

Congratulations, you've made to the last chapter. You're almost home.

So far on our journey to true wealth, we've learned that we need to change behavior and the way we think, communicate, and interact with others. We've learned that not everyone shares our vision, goals, and objectives, and when we lose sight of that, we increase the odds of failing to adequately communicate our true intentions and find fulfillment.

Worse, our failures frequently cause us to assign incorrect intentions to others when we fail to recognize and remember that we are all different and no two people ever share the same internal representations of the world.

We have set our intention to achieve true *wealth* and *prosperity*, and we've learned that first we need to identify what that means to us— it requires a definition.

We also learned that once we identified and adequately defined those terms, they had to be congruent with our values. If it falls short even just a little, it will sustain itself and you'll be disappointed or dissatisfied.

We all feel frustrations at work, personal, and social settings. When you have the time to reflect before you respond, you probably find yourself crafting your response slightly differently than if you had responded spontaneously without much thought, which usually is a good thing and results in far fewer apologies from all parties.

In a work setting, your success may very well depend on how your emotions control you as emotions are unconscious behaviors of values, beliefs, and patterns until they're not, becoming conscious patterns of behavior. You need to have your emotions working for you—not against you.

Self-awareness practiced through learning to take the time to discover yourself and how you respond when strong feelings or emotions are triggered will dramatically alter the filters and your interactions with others.

Over time and with practice, you will find that as you function on "auto-pilot," you will be less likely to allow your emotions to rule as you become the master of your emotions. Mastering this technique alone could cause a change from working in a job that you can't stand to transforming it into one you can't wait to get to.

Getting in touch with emotional self-awareness is no easy challenge. Throughout your day, take the time to stop and examine the following:

- Your breathing – Is it deep or shallow, fast or slow?

- Are you tense or relaxed?

- Are you comfortable, or do you have any discomfort in your body; if so, where?

- Can you describe your mental state – Are sleepy or tired, or are you alert?

The more you practice asking yourself these variables, the more in tune you will become with your feelings and emotions <u>in the moment</u>, providing you far greater control and a recognition of negative emotions, fear, anger, or frustration when they first move from your unconscious to your conscious state.

Filters define the world you live in and if left unchecked or unexamined, can create obstacles and roadblocks that become your reality—or **"your world."**

The filters through which we view and interact with those around us shape our perceptions. We use those perceptions to then mold the way we behave and decide to interact or, in many instances, whether we decide to interact at all. We also use them to measure ourselves and those around us.

The introspective strength one can gain from an honest assessment of their "world modeling" can be profound. For instance, if you go through life complaining and looking for excuses for behavior, results, or sub-par performance, you will continue to live your life that way because that's your world—it's perfectly normal to you.

Another way of looking at it would be if you go through life looking for problems, you won't have any trouble finding them. You will find problems because finding problems is your "goal."

However, if you go through life looking for quality, superiority, improvement, distinction, and excellence, you will find all of those and live a life of exceptional quality and excellence. Given the choice between these two goals, which one makes infinitely more sense?

By changing your filters, you have the ability to change YOUR world and in turn have a positive influence on those around you.

Many who go through life looking for problems don't realize that problems create dead ends and excuses. If you're inclined to look for what could go wrong and not focus on the other side of that equation (what will go right), you will most likely find yourself in a self-defeating mindset.

The first step is to remove the word "problem" from your vocabulary. Instead, make "problems" a "challenge" as challenges are meant to be overcome. There are solutions to challenges, while problems instill a subconscious barrier and a trigger toward defeat.

While everyone generally fears "failure," you can use that internal fear to your advantage. Think and accept that failure is nothing more than describing a result **YOU** didn't want.

Furthermore, **YOU** decide when failure begins and when it ends. Never let anyone tell you that you have failed. Perhaps you're just not done yet, because there is no such thing as failure—***just results from feedback.***

Make this transformation, examine your life filters, be proactive and make changes where needed. If you do, your challenges will seem trivial, and every letdown will become a learning experience.

Focus on excellence.

Focus determines your results. Many just focus on passing, just getting by. If this is your focus, what happens when you fall just 1% short of your goal? You fail!

What happens if you focus on excellence? If you achieve 90% of your goal, you're still in the "A" grade region, so you probably did great and are satisfied.

So at 90%, you did great even though you missed your goal by 10%.

Because you were just trying to get by, missing by 1% or more typically results in your failure.

Your goal and your ability to identify and set your goal at excellence gives you a focus of attention and allows you to excel. So how do you set your goal? Write it down, and make it real—something that demands your focus on a daily basis.

Identify incremental way points, and celebrate those achievements because they will reinforce your focus and keep you on track and on time to achieve your GOAL.

Stretch yourself, and make sure you leave your comfort zone to achieve your goal. Leaving your comfort zone demands and requires greater focus.

Have you ever found yourself really excited about a prospect, project, or upcoming life event only to have an unplanned, unforeseen obstacle present itself and sidetrack your dreams, goals, or vision? You're not alone in both experiencing these types of challenges or in how you decide to deal with or address them.

However, the vast majority of people who find themselves presented with these barriers or distractions far too often develop a mindset that precludes them from moving beyond them and finding solutions to their challenges.

Once the obstacle has been set, many people give up instead of using the challenge as a learning experience and discovering what, if anything, they could or should have done differently.

The barrier or challenge becomes invaluable *feedback,* a learning event designed to give you knowledge and, ultimately, choices. What you do with that knowledge will define whether you can master overcoming your life challenges or become a victim to them.

One doesn't have to look that far to find the disadvantaged—those who have given up and surrendered their lives to the wishes, beliefs, and mandates of others.

Learn to live your life on YOUR terms!

What's right for you is right for YOU. Don't be afraid of falling down from time to time. Use it as a learning experience and know that if you gave up as a young child, you'd never have learned to walk, or speak, or have become the wonderful, generous, and grateful person you are today.

How do I know that's you? Because you found and took the time to read this helpful book. Now it's your turn to extend OUR message of learning and choice.

Take the time to share this with someone special, someone you care deeply about. Together, don't be afraid to discuss and find solutions to life's challenges and ways around barriers.

The last critical element required for true *Wealth & Prosperity* is a sense of giving, a sense of charity. Whether it's of your time, your talent, or your money, giving back creates an overwhelming sense of personal gratitude.

It immediately changes your body chemistry and releases a feeling of joy and fulfillment. Don't be afraid to step out of your comfort zone and serve others less fortunate than you. Help them help themselves, and pass along some of the lessons you've learned.

How great would it feel to see a person, a family, an organization rise up to take command and control of their destinies, all because of the window of light you allowed to shine through?

Take these lessons to heart. Work on yourself so that those closest to you don't have to.

Dr. Matt James has a saying "Whether you think you can or you can't, you're right."

You already possess all the resources necessary; you just need to **Think & Grow Wealthy** as you marvel in your **Amazing Passage to Prosperity & Abundance.**

ABOUT THE AUTHOR

Robert "Bud" Heng holds a Bachelor's of Science degree in Management Science and has over 40 years of experience serving federal, state, and local law enforcement. He is a registered investment adviser representative for a Registered Investment Advisory firm and has passed his Series 7, 63 & 65 licensing exams. He is also a Certified Practitioner in Neuro-Linguistic-Programming, certified by and affiliated with the Association for Integrative Psychology. Robert through RH Counseling; provides counseling and coaching for corporate, law enforcement and individual clients -- helping achieve greater levels of awareness, wealth, control and empowerment through enhanced understanding and innovation in personal communication. You can find additional information at RH Counseling.